Baby Mickey Books and Shapes

A GOLDEN BOOK • NEW YORK
Western Publishing Company, Inc., Racine, Wisconsin 53404

Baby Mickey has lost his ball. It is his favorite toy. He wants to find it.

Baby Mickey crawls away to look for the
ball. Where can it be?

Baby Mickey sees a *triangle* shape. Is that his ball?

No. It is the sail of Baby Donald's toy boat.

"Ball?" says Baby Mickey. He wants to know if Baby Donald has his ball.

"Boat!" says Baby Donald. The boat is the only toy he has.

He goes with Baby Mickey to find Baby Mickey's ball.

Baby Mickey and Baby Donald see a *star* shape. What is it?

It is Baby Minnie's pinwheel.

"Ball?" say Baby Mickey and Baby Donald.

"Pinwheel!" says Baby Minnie. She has not seen the ball.

Baby Minnie goes with them to look for
Baby Mickey's ball.

There is a *square* shape. That is not Baby Mickey's toy.

It is the top block on Baby Daisy's block tower.

"Ball?" say Baby Mickey, Baby Donald, and Baby Minnie.

"Block!" says Baby Daisy.

Baby Daisy goes along to find Baby Mickey's ball.

There is an *oval* shape. What is it?

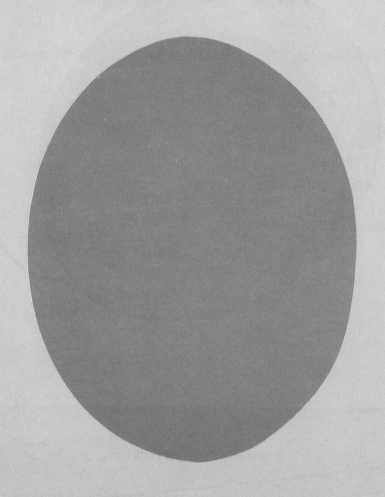

It is Baby Goofy's balloon.

"Ball?" say Baby Mickey, Baby Donald,
Baby Minnie, and Baby Daisy.
"Balloon!" says Baby Goofy.
Baby Goofy follows along.

They see something *round.* Is that Baby Mickey's ball?

Yes, it is! Baby Pluto is playing with it.
Now the friends play together. They share
the boat with the *triangle* sail, the *star*-shaped
pinwheel, the *square* blocks, the *oval* balloon,
and the *round* ball.

Then the friends take their toys and
go home.

Baby Mickey waves good-by. He is happy.
He has found his *round* ball.